AVOID DECEPTION AND WALK IN THE LIGHT

A GUIDE FOR CHRISTIANS IN THIS CHALLENGING WORLD

MINISTER SHENOA T. GIBSON

AVOID DECEPTION AND WALK IN THE LIGHT
A GUIDE FOR CHRISTIANS IN THIS CHALLENGING WORLD

iUniverse books may be ordered through booksellers or by contacting:

iUniverse
1663 Liberty Drive
Bloomington, IN 47403
www.iuniverse.com
844-349-9409

Because of the dynamic nature of the Internet, any web addresses or links contained in this book may have changed since publication and may no longer be valid. The views expressed in this work are solely those of the author and do not necessarily reflect the views of the publisher, and the publisher hereby disclaims any responsibility for them.

Any people depicted in stock imagery provided by Getty Images are models, and such images are being used for illustrative purposes only.
Certain stock imagery © Getty Images.

ISBN: 978-1-6632-5654-6 (sc)
ISBN: 978-1-6632-5655-3 (e)

Library of Congress Control Number: 2023918119

Print information available on the last page.

iUniverse rev. date: 10/09/2023

CONTENTS

CONTENTS

DEDICATION

To my immediate and extended family, I love you all!

My mother, Evangelist Valerie Jackson, you have inspired me to be the best me I can be in Christ. You are a godly example of what a woman of God is. I am proud to be the daughter of such an anointed and talented songbird of God.

I thank God for my sister. Jackie, you are a gifted and talented woman blessed by God. I thank the Lord for my younger brother, Will, and his wife, Angela. I appreciate your continued support in all I do and being loved by you while we all grow in the grace and knowledge of Christ.

To my sons, DeJuan and Jalen Carter, you are my heart, and I thank God for you. I strive to be the best mother I can be for you. I keep you covered in prayer that God will allow you to flourish into the men that His will purposes for you.

To my love, Daniel, thank you for being you. You are such a loving supporter of my gifts, talents, and calls that God has entrusted me with. I thank God that He connected me with a person who allows me to be who God called and is calling me to be with no hesitation. God truly gave me a gift when He placed you and Nigel in my life.

To Jesus, as the song says, "I choose you again and again," and dedicate my life and this book to You. I pray that You will be pleased with the work I am doing for You. I pray that it will draw men and women to You now and for years to come if You delay Your return.

PREFACE

In this book, I share a topic that has grieved my heart. My husband, Daniel, and I went through a situation at church that shook us and caused us to ponder the state of this world and how the Bible is unfolding before our eyes.

I am sure you may be curious about what could have happened that would cause us such grief. What I will share is that we heard a preached message from a pastor we respected. He disclosed at the beginning of the message that this was one that would be controversial and may cause questions and even division in the church. The message had a beautiful title and a vision of how we are all God's children. Sounds great, don't you think? Well, the problem was that this beautiful message knitted truths and compromise. A seemingly firm stand on God's Word in one statement and a contradiction in the next. We were stunned to hear a message of this kind coming from one we looked to for the preached, uncompromised Word of God. We listened to the message more than once with our Bibles in hand, comparing notes, and discussing our findings. Lord, no! This can't be!

Did we just experience a sermon weaved with devices of the enemy? Were souls being misled and at ease in sinful living? "My heart, Lord, it hurts. I wonder how your heart feels Lord," I pray for this pastor! This brought tears to my eyes, as it is doing even as I write this. The burden to stand for truth and for Jesus Christ felt and *still* feels so heavy.

Have you ever had a family and friends gathering? Food was being served there. Not just *any* food, but *your* favorite menu items. Since we are imagining, there are no calories, judgments, or health constraints involved, so think of your favorite meal for a moment. I'm envisioning my plate with macaroni and cheese with at least five cheeses, sweet potato casserole with a sweet glaze of buttery goodness and crunchy topping for texture, and kale and collard greens mixed, which cuts the bitterness of the collards. Yum! How about some good ole stuffing with cranberry sauce and gravy, and a piece of hot-off-the-grill, well-seasoned chicken breast? Don't forget you can wash all this yumminess down with a glass of homemade sweet tea. Is your mouth salivating yet? What a delectable plate! You are ready to dig in. You cut into the chicken, anxious to eat it, and find it is raw inside. The juice from the raw chicken has now flowed throughout your entire plate. What happens to all that good food? It is now contaminated by raw meat juice.

What may contaminate my meal may not be the same as what contaminates or ruins yours. Imagine that just happened to your meal. Maybe dirt was thrown on your plate, or you found bugs crawling on your plate, or long strands of hair are on the plate. You get the picture.

That was how the sermon was served. Truths were the plate of yummy goodness, and the contamination and compromise were the raw chicken and juice—or any other elements that made the food inedible—were flowing all over the plate. Now the meal is ruined! And you are now at risk of becoming ill if you eat anything on the plate. We must be careful to ensure what we allow into our spirits is good for us and not contaminated.

We had many conversations about how the enemy of our souls is seeping into the church, and how we, as Christians, are to move through challenging situations in this day. As we continued our conversations, Daniel looked at me and said, "You should write a book about this." Little did I know that the deep conversations, prayers, and scriptures were preparing me to write this Bible-based book in such a short time. Four days, in my opinion, is a short time. I am so fortunate to have received such wonderful support from Daniel and my mother during this time.

For years, there has been talk of Jesus's return. We are the closest we have ever been to that happy day. I want, no ... wait ... I *need* to do my part in helping people everywhere become aware of the impacts deception has on us and what God's Word says about it. I have seen warnings on social media and preached messages on how deception is rising rapidly but seems to be missed by even the saints of God. Unfortunately, I have seen it personally. I believe God wants us to know how to avoid deception, and this book will do just that *if* you take the time to read and apply the concepts to your everyday life. This is a good time to grab some things as you read this book. Your Holy Bible (choose your favorite version and platform; I use the Amplified and King James versions in this book), favorite pen, paper, sticky notes, highlighters, and/or laptop. Whatever items you use to engage in study and taking notes.

Some may wonder, what makes me an authority on the subject or even to give a warning to those in ministry and the body of Christ. Thank you for wondering. I am a dedicated child of God and a minister of the Gospels of Jesus Christ through Christian Global Outreach Ministry since 2018. I am the founder of Dare Two Pray Ministry since 2019, and the author of *Simple Steps to Salvation and Effective Prayer* (available on all digital platforms). In addition, I have experienced deception. Not that any of these matter in God's eyes. I believe He is directing me, and I want to be obedient to God and follow His leading to serve the body of Christ in the way He graces me to.

I am working to please the Lord and am being led to be a vessel by using my words on paper to reach the world about the topic of deception. The purpose of this book is to enlighten, expose, and encourage. I pray it blesses you as writing it has blessed me.

OPENING PRAYER

Let prayer proceed all we do.

Dear Heavenly Father,

I come to You as humbly as I know how, asking You to use this book to reach the masses. Allow the words that are contained in this book be a way to illuminate the minds and hearts of Your people. Lord, I ask that You anoint this book so that every reader will feel Your presence, receive/retain salvation, be restored to right standing, turn from wickedness, and live holy and acceptable unto You. Let this book glorify You, Lord! I pray that the enemy's schemes and plans are canceled and that divine revelation takes place. I pray that any confusion be undone and that Your Holy Word will go forth expressly. I pray that the topic of this book will be well received and that lives will be changed by your Holy Ghost and fire!

I pray the content in this book is clear and shows Your love for us and will draw people to the cross. I pray that anyone not exposed to the Gospel of Jesus Christ will hear the message and accept You as Lord in their lives. I pray they have access to the Holy Bible in the regions in which they live so they can learn of You.

I thank You in advance, and You get all the glory! In Jesus's name I pray. Amen.

INTRODUCTION

Have you ever been in a situation where you felt like you had been deceived, hoodwinked, bamboozled?

Have you ever been in a place where you thought what was being said was correct, only later find out that it was not, and you have been misled?

Have you ever seen a card trick? "Pick a card, any card," says the person doing the trick. You pick a card, and the person then "magically" has the card you picked in his or her hands. With a sleight of hand manipulation of the deck, you can be tricked into believing that the illusion or trick is real. You may even be in awe as to how it was done.

I wonder if you have ever shopped online and seen the perfect item. I have! I purchased a swimsuit online because I was going on vacation. This swimsuit was perfect! The shoulder straps were wide enough for me, the fringed cover-up bottom allowed me to remain modest, and the color was a vibrant blue. This suit was all I wanted because it would allow me to be comfortable even though I am not one for bathing suits. But that is a whole different book. When the item arrived, oh my, it was not at all what I ordered! It was three sizes too small, it was three weeks late, and the blue looked as if someone sucked all the vibrancy out during the shipment! What was I to do? Well, I went somewhere else to get what I needed that fit me and gave me the same comfort I needed to even step foot in public wearing that type of garment.

You may be wondering why I am referencing times of deception, being misled, and not getting what you need. Although my story may have caused a giggle—I hope it did, anyway—a much more serious topic will be covered as we proceed through the remainder of this book.

Deception! In this day and time, we are consumed by many things that can draw our focus and cause us to be led astray and deceived. It is time to uncover the enemy's plan for our souls and run to the covering of our God and Lord, Jesus Christ. Deception is not a recent phenomenon. It began in the garden of Eden.

The book of Genesis talks about the fall of Adam. If you allow me to paraphrase, what follows is an abridged version of the story. Adam was commanded not to eat from the tree of the knowledge of good and evil because they would surely die. But the serpent—the devil—then went to Eve and told her she would not surely die; she would become like God. Eve ate the fruit from the forbidden tree and gave some to Adam. He from the tree too, which caused severe consequences.

The serpent in the conversation with Eve was cunning and mixed some truth with a lie. It is interesting that the serpent went to Eve, as God had not given her the command not to eat from the forbidden tree. Adam was responsible for his disobedience because he received the command directly from God. Because of deception and disobedience, we were separated from God. As you keep reading, you will see why we need to be enlightened and walk in the light to avoid deception.

DEFINING DECEPTION

In this chapter, we define what deception means and what it means to be deceived. Throughout this book, you may see familiar terms and terms that may be new to you. Terms may be used interchangeably, so synonyms are included to ensure you have the entire perspective as you continue to read and become more enlightened. I present the information in this manner so that even the novice will understand and be able to apply this information to life and circumstances.

Take a moment to define in your own words what the word *deception* means:

_____

_____

_____

Now, let's see how it is "officially" defined.

According to *Merriam-Webster*, the definition of deception is as follows:

- The act of causing someone to accept as true or valid what is false or invalid: the act of *deceiving*
- The fact or condition of being deceived
- Something that deceives: trick

Synonyms and words relative to deception include:

- Fraud—always implies guilt and often criminality in act or practice.
- Double-dealing—suggests treachery or at least action contrary to a professed attitude.
- Trickery—implies ingenious acts intended to dupe or cheat.

- Subterfuge—the adoption of a stratagem or telling of a lie in order to escape guilt or to gain an end.
- Stratagem—an artifice or trick in war for deceiving and outwitting the enemy, cleverly contrived trick or scheme for gaining an end, skill in ruses or trickery.
- Manipulation—to control or play upon by artful, unfair, or insidious means especially to one's own advantage.
- Perfidious—the quality or state of being faithless or disloyal: treachery.
  o My mom was unaware of this word and the Holy Spirit led her to it. She shared this word and how this relates to the word deception.
- Imposter—a person who is not what he or she pretends to be.

Did your definition match what was officially given?

As you may gather from defining deception, it is not a good thing, to say the least. Why would anyone want to be deceived or use divisive tactics when dealing with others? What is to be gained by dealing so underhandedly? What would be the intent in one's heart to be part of such an evil scheme?

I know the examples I gave earlier do not seem to be so harmful. You can always go to the store and get a new garment. You may even know there is a form of illusion or deception when viewing what seems to be as innocent as a cute card trick. Is this serious? Does this have weight today? I am glad you asked!

Yes! What seems to be innocent can be an entry point to larger plots and schemes of the enemy of our souls. The enemy is Satan, the one cast down from heaven, and as the Bible says, "your adversary the devil, roaring as a lion, walking about, seeking whom he may devour" (Peter 5:8 KJV).

In 2022, I had a dream that was scary yet encouraging. I was on a highway at night, and the lanes split in two. There were so many people on the highway. People in blindfolds were almost shoulder-to-shoulder as they went down the left side of the wider road. They were walking like zombies. You know, like in the movies, their hands extended as they tried to feel their way around. The Bible calls it groping in darkness as if blinded. I was standing on the narrow side of the highway under a beautiful bright light near the edge of the road. As people walked toward the split in the road, they had to choose to continue down the wider highway or go to the right, narrower road with the light. I saw people decide to go toward the narrow road. As they ran to get off the wide road, the blindfolds dropped off, and they could see they were now moving in the right direction. They seemed happy and filled with excitement as they began to see the light. It was scary to see how many were still lost and going down the wide road. But it was encouraging because it was not too late for people to choose the way of the light.

This reminds me of Matthew 7:13–14 (KJV) "Enter ye in at the strait gate: for wide is the gate, and broad is the way, that leadeth to destruction, and many there be which go in there at: Because strait is the gate, and *narrow* is the way, which leadeth unto life, and few there be that find it."

I believe that dream is what is happening now. So many people are blinded by false teachings and prosperity messages with no correction or teaching of biblical principles to apply to life. Compromising biblical principles are used to increase social media following numbers and church member attendance. Not to mention the wide acceptance of sinful living. People walk aimlessly and confidently in the wrong direction, which leads to hell. Some may not believe what they see or read is that bad. For example, like that cute card trick I spoke about earlier. It may seem cute to watch a small trick a kid may play. But remember, you can be lured into practicing witchcraft by trying trivial things like buying artifacts such as Harry Potter wands, dream catchers, and crystals. These things may seem harmless, but they open portals to darkness. I have heard about people who enjoyed watching *Harry Potter* and even *The Craft* movies and later started practicing witchcraft.

Let me say that I have nothing against entertainment. I also know that what we consume with our eyes and ears can certainly be a launch pad to other thoughts and practices. Eventually, you can become entangled in things contrary to God's Word that you never thought you would try. I know this is hard to hear, but we must be watchful and aware of anything that can become a snare, throw us off track, and put us on the wrong side of the road.

In the dream, I believe the light shining on me was a representation of Jesus Christ, the Light of the world. He does not want anyone to perish but to come into the full knowledge of Him to gain life eternal in heaven.

As a child of God and believer in Jesus Christ, I have noticed that so many are being deceived and moving away from biblically sound doctrine and teachings. This creates such a deep concern in me for this world. The Bible speaks of a great "falling away," and I never thought I would see it in my day.

Studies Show Christians Are Leaving the Faith

On July 27, 2022, I saw a study on a blog by Dirk Rinker and Michael Jaffarian that said many are leaving the faith, which the Bible said would happen. Here are some additional findings:

> When asked what their religion is, 64.2% of Americans will say "Christian."

> In the past ten years, fifteen million Americans left the Christian faith. This is not just about people getting more lax about church attendance, drifting away but still believing in Jesus, still considering Christianity to be their faith. No. This is about people saying, "I was a Christian ten years ago, but now I'm not." The number of sheep leaving the fold is greater than the number of sheep coming into it.

Fifteen million is not a small number. It hurts my heart to know people are turning away from truth and hope. As stated, more people are leaving than coming to Christ. I was talking to God, and authoring this book is *my* way of doing what I can to share the love of Jesus and to give hope to a world that is lost and in a dark place full of falsities and deceptions that lead people away from God. It is my prayer that God will use this book to enlighten the minds of the people and infuse hope.

THE IMPORTANCE OF LIGHT

What happens when you come home and turn on a light? Its illumination uncovers and exposes. It shows the rooms, the décor, the flooring, and so on. It also exposes the dust and dirt, the stains on the carpets, the broken seals on the windows, and the leftovers on the kitchen countertops. It can also uncover an intruder who snuck into your home unbeknown to you, stealing your personal belongings. Turning on the light can be exciting as you see the beauty of your home. It can be overwhelming if there is a lot of cleaning to do. And it can also be comforting to know that you are safe, secure, and at peace.

Who really wants to sit in the dark? I'll give you one guess … the ruler of darkness. The enemy of our souls wants us to remain in darkness. Who wants to be in a place where he or she feels there is neither hope nor access to light? When you are in the dark, you cannot identify the dangers lurking around you.

Take a minute to face something that some may want to avoid, like sitting in the dangers of the dark. You can overcome the darkness. The enemy wants to prey on those who are in darkness or are weak. The greatest deception is the enemy who convinces people that he is light. That he has what you need. That believing in Christ does nothing for you. Prayer is of no effect.

Today is a new day! Invite Jesus to abide in your home. Jesus is the Light!

When Jesus is in your home, darkness must flee. The enemy must go! Light and darkness have no fellowship. The Bible says in John 1:5 (AMP), "The light shines-in the darkness, and the darkness did not understand it or overpower it or appropriate it or absorb it {and is unreceptive to it}." Light is powerful and needed. Having the Light is important. Here are the benefits of having the Light of Jesus:

It exposes us. It shows nooks and crannies of sin hiding in our lives and areas of threats that need attention. When the light is on, you can see the areas in your life that need to be cleaned and changed, or trash that needs to be taken to the garbage. By taking inventory of your life and how you are living, you acknowledge that you need to empty yourself of all the things contrary to the life Christ wants you to live. Psalm 139:23–24 (KJV) tells us, "Search me, O God, and know my heart; Try me and know my thoughts; And see if there be any wicked way in me and lead me in the way everlasting." And Romans 6:23(KJV) says, "For the wages of sin is death; but the gift of God is eternal life through Jesus Christ our Lord."

It saves us. When we call to Jesus, He will save us. Through prayer, we can talk to the Lord and accept Him as our Savior. God loves us so much that He gave His only Son to die for us. "For whosoever shall call upon the name of the Lord shall be saved" Romans 10:13 (KJV).

It cleanses us. Jesus will cleanse you from all unrighteousness. The remarkable thing is that you do not have to clean up yourself. All the work is done through your acceptance of Jesus. You are sanctified, made holy. You are justified or seen as holy in the sight of God. Psalm 51:10 (KJV) reads, "Create in me a clean heart, O God; And renew the right spirit within me."

It protects us. It shuts down the dangers lurking around you. God is our protector. We have the Lord as our shelter and our fortress. We are covered from evil if we stay near to God. We do not have to fear because of this assurance.

> He shall cover thee with his feathers, and under his wings shalt though trust: His truth shall be thy shield and buckler. Thou shalt not be afraid for the

terror by night; Nor for the arrow that flieth by day; Nor for the pestilence that walketh in darkness; Nor for the destruction that wasteth at noonday. Psalm 91:4–6 (KJV)

It seals us. It joins you with Christ so that nothing can separate you. We are sealed, which refers to being connected or joined to Christ after we accept Him as Savior. When you seal tightly, nothing can get between you and the Lord. "For I am persuaded, that neither death, nor life, nor angels, nor principalities, nor powers, nor things present, nor things to come: Nor height, nor depth, nor any other creature, shall be able to separate us from the love of God, which is in Christ Jesus our Lord" Romans 8:38–39 (KJV).

Darkness cannot remain when Jesus is present. Isn't that great news? You have hope in Jesus, and you become the light of the world because Jesus will shine through you!

Take a minute to write down your thoughts about how knowing the benefits of light will help you:

_____

_____

_____

Prayer of Salvation

Before we continue, I want to give you the opportunity to accept the Lord Jesus Christ as your personal Savior today. Please say this prayer, based on Romans chapter 10, with me:

> Dear Jesus,
>
> I ask for forgiveness of my sins. I repent (turn away) from living in sin. I believe You came to save the world from sin by dying on the cross. I believe You rose again on the third day. I confess with my mouth that Jesus, You are Lord. I choose You, Jesus, this day and will serve You with all my heart and allow Your light to shine through me. Lord, fill me with Your precious Holy Spirit that will be my comfort and my guide. I pray that all barriers that attempt to hinder me from walking in Your light will be destroyed. In Jesus's name, I praise You and thank You, Jesus. Amen.

Hallelujah! The angels in heaven are rejoicing now that you have accepted Jesus into your heart.

Please record the date you said this prayer and declared Jesus as your Savior _____/_____/_____.

The angels in heaven are rejoicing right now! Praise and glory to God!

WHAT THE BIBLE SAYS ABOUT DECEPTION

The Bible is the Living Word. What I mean by this is that we are privileged to have access to what God has to say about historical events and what is to come. The Bible is filled with prophetic messages that help us along the way, warning us to avoid being deceived. This is what we need today. Heed the voice and the Word of the Lord. The Word of God is a lamp unto my feet and a light to my pathway.

Here is what the Bible says about deception. Please highlight and take notes on what resonates with you in this portion of the book:

The Bible says in Matthew 24:24 (KJV), "For there shall arise false Christs, and false prophets, and shall shew great signs and wonders; insomuch that, if it were possible, they shall deceive the very elect."

This scripture shows that even those who believe in Jesus Christ, those referred to as "the very elect," and are living for him are susceptible to deception if not alert and aware of the enemy's devices. In 2 Corinthians 2:11 (KJV), the Bible says, "Lest Satan should get an advantage of us: for we are not ignorant of his devices." God has given us the Word of God to learn from, to become enlightened and aware of the devices and strategies of the enemy.

There will be those who claim the name of Christ and be used as instruments of manipulation. The enemy is at work, and we must be able to identify those who are rising as false prophets.

> Now in regard to the coming of our Lord Jesus Christ and our gathering together to *meet* Him, we ask you, brothers and sisters, not to be quickly unsettled or alarmed either by a [so-called prophetic revelation of a] spirit or a message or a letter [alleged to be] from us to the effect that the day of the Lord has [already] come. Let no one in any way

deceive *or* entrap you, for *that day will not come* unless the apostasy comes first [that is, the great rebellion, the abandonment of the faith by professed Christians], and the man of lawlessness is revealed, the son of destruction [the Antichrist, the one who is destined to be destroyed] 2 Thessalonians 2:1–3 (AMP).

In the book of 2 Thessalonians, Paul, the writer, references future events. The rapture of believers is also referred to as the "catching away" of the saints of God. There is a day when false Christs will rise and say the Lord has already come. We are not to be deceived. As you see in this scripture, the falling away has started as was noted in an earlier chapter and even in my dream.

> On the contrary, it is you who is wrong and defraud, and you do this even to your brothers and sisters. Do you not know that the unrighteous will not inherit *or* have any share in the kingdom of God? Do not be deceived; neither the sexually immoral, nor idolaters, nor adulterers, nor effeminate [by perversion], nor those who participate in homosexuality,[10] nor thieves, nor the greedy, nor drunkards, nor revilers [whose words are used as weapons to abuse, insult, humiliate, intimidate, or slander], nor swindlers will inherit *or* have any share in the kingdom of God. 1 Corinthians 6:8–10 (AMP)

Write down anything that stands out to you in this section.

_____

_____

_____

This scripture wants us to see that when we live in a way not pleasing to God, our souls are in jeopardy. We will not inherit the kingdom of God. We cannot be deceived into believing that we can be just "good people" or live in ways that are contrary to the ways God wants us to live and still expect to see Jesus in peace and go to heaven.

Today you may hear people—possibly including people leaving the faith, preachers, teachers, and those who want to distort the truth to form an acceptance of sinful living—say that God is love, and He wants you just as you are. This is true. But wait, there is more! God *is* love. That is a biblical concept. He showed His love, as previously mentioned, by sending His Son, Jesus, to bear the sins of the world. God has requirements. He requires us to love Him and serve Him with all our hearts. The Bible says in Romans 12:1 (AMP), "Therefore I urge you, brothers and sisters, by the mercies of God, to present your bodies [dedicating all of yourselves, set apart] as a living sacrifice, holy and well-pleasing to God, *which is* your rational (logical, intelligent) act of worship". We are to live a wonderful life in worship of our God so we can live again in heavenly places.

We Have Hope

This is why the Light is so important. We are contending with a cunning and deceitful enemy who wants us to be confused, tricked, led astray, and feel like we are all alone.

> Beware of false prophets, which come to you in sheep's clothing, but inwardly they are ravening wolves. Ye shall know them by their fruits. Do men gather grapes of thorns, or figs of thistles? Even so every good tree bringeth forth good fruit; but a corrupt tree bringeth forth evil fruit. A good tree cannot bring forth evil fruit, neither can a corrupt tree bring forth good fruit. Matthew 7:15–18 (KJV)

I know most of these scriptures reference prophets. *Why are prophets so important?* you may be wondering. Why are they so key to understanding the enemy's plan or God's plan? What does the office of the prophet do?

Prophets are vocal ambassadors of the Most High God. They work by the unction of the Holy Ghost. They play integral parts in carrying information to the people. The prophets do not just tell the future or give "a word" to someone in church. They are key in planting the Word of God in the hearts of the people. Prophets will warn, guide, encourage, intercede, teach, and provide counsel. They will bring the pure Word of God to people and call people to respond to the Word given. As the scripture says, you will know them by their fruit or what they produce. This is why it is so important to watch for those who are not working in the truth that leads to Jesus. We are not to be confused or used by those who are imposters, medians, fortune tellers, and the like. They may have a "gift" to foretell, but how are they guiding you, and where is the information coming from?

The kingdom of darkness has those who work as well. When the Holy Spirit is moving and speaking, even the workers of darkness will acknowledge that only God is able to know those things or perform such miracles. They will recognize the Light of the world!

You will see the book of Ezekiel is filled with such a move of God and how God can use us in a mighty way to build faith and save souls from the enemy. If I may paraphrase one excerpt, Moses was told by God that he would confront Pharaoh, the leader of Egypt, and tell him to let God's people go. It took various miracles and plagues to get Pharaoh's attention. He had magicians and sorcerers come and try to duplicate the miracles God told Moses to perform. There came a point when those who worked in magic could not duplicate what God did. They had to bow to the Most High God and admit that the miracles performed could only be done by the God of Moses.

I know this may be a biblical reference, but it is just as relevant today. There is no match for our God and His divine power! We have the victory through Christ!

A WARNING TO FALSE PROPHETS AND PASTORS

Ministry is vital, and our faith leaders are invaluable in providing the necessary care and guidance for the body of Christ and the community. Bishops, prophets, and church leaders have a huge responsibility. Effective and godly leaders are imperative in making sure the church stays connected to the Holy Spirit.

The enemy has crept into many of today's churches. So many churches willingly compromise biblical principles to gain attendance, fame, and money. I have witnessed a church promote acceptance of sinful behavior and not share what God's Word says about living willfully in sin and its consequences. Heaven is real. So is hell.

The desire to not confront this complex world of demonic oppression and doctrines will lead people down a path of destruction. The Bible is clear about such issues and warns our leaders to stay close to God and refrain from any evildoings with malicious intent. Please read the book of Ezekiel, beginning with the excerpt that follows, to learn how God feels about prophets who deal in lies.

Take a moment to read this scripture. Use your highlighter, and take some notes:

> And the word of the Lord came to me saying, "Son of man, prophesy against the prophets of Israel who prophesy, and say to those who prophesy from their own inspiration, 'Hear the word of the Lord!' Thus says the Lord God, "Woe (judgment is coming) to the foolish prophets who are following their own spirit [claiming to have seen things] but have [in fact] seen nothing. O Israel, your prophets have been like foxes among the ruins. You

have not gone up into the gaps *or* breaches, nor built the wall around the house of Israel that it might stand in the battle on the day of the Lord. They have seen falsehood and lying divination, saying, 'The Lord says,' but the Lord has not sent them. Yet they hope *and* make men to hope for the confirmation of their word. Did you not see (make up) a false vision and speak a lying divination when you said, 'The Lord declares,' but it is not I who have spoken?'"

Therefore, thus says the Lord God, "Because you have spoken empty *and* delusive words and have seen lies, therefore behold, I am against you," says the Lord God. "So My hand will be against the [counterfeit] prophets who see (make up) empty *and* delusive visions and who give lying prophecies. They will have no place in the [secret] council of My people, nor will they be recorded in the register of the house of Israel, nor will they enter the land of Israel, that you may know [without any doubt] that I am the Lord God. Ezekiel 13 (AMP)

What stands out to you in this scripture text?

_____

_____

_____

This scripture shows that pastors must be careful, or God will be displeased or even, dare I say, be angry, and consequences will be in store for them.

"Woe to the shepherds (civil leaders, rulers) who are destroying and scattering the sheep of My pasture!" says the Lord. Therefore thus says the Lord, the God of Israel, in regard to the shepherds who care for *and* feed My people: "You have scattered My flock and driven them away, and have not attended to them; hear this, I am about to visit *and* attend to you for the evil of your deeds," says the Lord. Jeremiah 23:1–2 (AMP)

As you can see, God does not tolerate leaders of the body of Christ who mistreat and mislead us. Pastors are to be caring about the Father's work. They must not scatter the flock by contaminating the Word of God by mixing truths with lies, dealing underhandedly with funds, allowing the ministry to adopt doctrines of evil, and the like. God is love, and He left these examples in the Word for us to review so we can avoid punishment for this behavior.

Now let us look at our example of the "Good Shepherd":

> I am the Good Shepherd. The Good Shepherd lays down His [own] life for the sheep. But the hired man [who merely serves for wages], who is neither the shepherd nor the owner of the sheep, when he sees the wolf coming, deserts the flock and runs away; and the wolf snatches the sheep and scatters them. The man runs because he is a hired hand [who serves only for wages] and is not concerned about the [safety of the] sheep. John 10:11–13 (AMP)

In this passage, we see that Jesus is the "Good Shepherd." He died for our sins. Many people are hired and appointed as bishops, pastors, and leaders in the church. And while they serve, their hearts are not of God. Some are out for nothing but monetary gain.

> This is a true saying, if a man desire the office of a bishop, he desireth a good work. A bishop then must be blameless, the husband of one wife, vigilant, sober, of good behaviour, given to hospitality, apt to teach; Not given to wine, no striker, not greedy of *filthy lucre* (gaining money in a dishonorable way); but patient, not a brawler, not covetous; One that ruleth well his own house, having his children in subjection with all gravity; (For if a man know not how to rule his own house, how shall he take

care of the church of God?) Not a novice, lest being lifted
up with pride he falls into the condemnation of the devil.
1 Timothy 3:1–6 (KJV

Hiring preachers *without consulting God* has consequences. Jesus wants to
make sure we have leaders after His own heart. Shepherds are protectors
and guides for the sheep. They will not allow them to be led to destruction
or be devoured.

There is a song that comes to mind that shows us the passion Christ has
for us. It is "Reckless Love," by Cory Asbury.

Take a moment to write down a song or scripture that resonates and
reminds you of God's divine and true love for us:

_____

_____

_____

_____

God cares for us, loves us, and wants us to be under His divine protection,
safe from the wolves and the adversary. If you have not noticed, I will say
it again: Jesus loves you. Research shows that the average person needs
to hear a message at least three times and up to thirty times to retain the
message. Repetition is essential in learning. I want this message to stick!

HOW FEAR CONNECTS WITH DECEPTION

In the beginning, we defined deception as the act of causing someone to accept as true or valid what is false or invalid. Fear also allows one to accept what is not truthful or valid. Fear is an uneasiness of mind upon the thought of future evil likely to befall us. This type of deception is within us. This type of manipulation is a type of spiritual warfare. We continually fight an invisible battle in our spirits and minds that swings into the realm of deception.

Did you know that fear is one way truth is distorted? People tend to build up thoughts that lead to anxiety due to the anticipated likelihood that something potentially bad, unfortunate, and traumatizing will happen. Fear amplifies thoughts and paralyzes actions. For example, when a person feels pain, he or she may be fearful and become mentally paralyzed but not make a doctor's appointment. Others make appointments to go to the doctor but can become fearful of what the pain may be, which may lead to stress and anxiety over what the diagnosis could be. Thoughts swirl in their minds, and fear may overtake them. But once the doctor's appointment is over, they realize that all the fear and anxiety were for naught. There was no significant issue. The mind is powerful, and when fear comes into play, truth is overridden by emotional responses.

List some ways that you stay grounded when negative thoughts and fear grip you and their benefits:

_____

_____

_____

_____

We must declare fear is canceled! Let us use the scriptures to keep our minds and hearts grounded so we can dispel lies and distorted truths caused by fear. You are victorious! The truth shall set us free.

Following are some scriptures that can help you.

When you feel alone, remember:

> Yea, though I walk through the valley of the shadow of death, I will fear no evil: for thou art with me; thy rod and thy staff they comfort me. (Psalm 23:4)

When you feel overwhelmed, remember:

> Be careful for nothing; but in every thing by prayer and supplication with thanksgiving let your requests be made known unto God. And the peace of God, which passeth all understanding, shall keep your hearts and minds through Christ Jesus. I can do all things through Christ which strengtheneth me. Philippians 4:6–8, 13 (KJV)

When you have forgotten that Jesus loves you, remember:

> There is no fear in love; but perfect love casteth out fear: because fear hath torment. He that feareth is not made perfect in love. 1 John 8:18 (KJV)

When you feel the battle is over, remember:

> Ye shall not fear them: for the Lord your God he shall fight for you. Deuteronomy 3:22 (KJV)

> Fear thou not; for I am with thee: be not dismayed; for I am thy God: I will strengthen thee; yea, I will help thee; yea, I will uphold thee with the right hand of my righteousness. Isaiah 41:10 (KJV)

When your thoughts become saturated with negativity, remember:

> Let this mind be in you, which was also in Christ Jesus. Philippians 2:5 (KJV)

> Finally, brethren, whatsoever things are true, whatsoever things are honest, whatsoever things are just, whatsoever things are pure, whatsoever things are lovely, whatsoever things are of good report; if there be any virtue, and if there be any praise, think on these things. Philippians 4:8 (KJV)

When the enemy tries to deceive you and cause you to feel powerless through fear and confusion, remember:

> For God hath not given us the spirit of fear; but of power, and of love, and of a sound mind. 2 Timothy 1:7 (KJV)

Knowledge and faith in God empower us to mute the voices of our fears. When we learn of God, we can battle the enemy and live in peace and truth. We can apply these scriptures and any others you may find in the Word of God daily to fight off the enemy's arrows of fear. Use the "sword of the Spirit" (Word of God) to fight and cut through all the mental negativity and emotional turmoil that comes our way during challenging moments in our lives. God loves us and wants us to cast our cares on Him because He cares for us. As stated previously, fear distorts the truth. With God's Word and protections, He allows us to discern truth and honesty.

YOUR RESPONSIBILITY AS A CHILD OF GOD

Sisters and brothers, we cannot leave the leaders of the body of Christ all the responsibility to avoid deception and living life contrary to how God wants us to live.

As I think of our role in this world, what comes to my mind is making a purchase. Yes, another purchase, but not a swimsuit this time. Instead, we purchase a dinner table. The box provides us with a photo of the finished product after it is assembled. We take out all the contents of the box and begin to build the table. Will the photo on the box of the complex item with no directions help you assemble it? It may help you get started, but you are also missing necessary information. The photo will not provide instructions about what screw goes in what place? We must read the instructions to get the details necessary for the table to be sturdy and ready for use. But remember, there are no instructions. Now for those handy folks who can look at a photo and assemble the item, go along with my analogy. You get the picture.

The Bible is our instruction book. Details found there give us explicit instructions on how to live a holy life free from sin and shame. We know that if we stray, the Bible will show us how to get back on track. If we are living according to His will, it shows us how to continue. If we are discouraged, we receive encouragement. We are warned about the consequences of sin. We cannot only rely on the preaching of the leaders to give us the Word of God. We must do what the Bible says in 2 Timothy 2:15 (KJV): "Study to shew thyself approved unto God, a workman that needeth not to be ashamed, rightly dividing the word of truth." We must study the Bible ourselves. Let us not manipulate ourselves into thinking we don't have to read the Word of God, that we can just listen to the pastors or teachers. We may also say, "I know enough of the Word."

During the pandemic, some churches were closed, and you could not enter. Where will you hear the Word if you do not take time to dive in yourself? I know online churches have become popular, but I reiterate that you must read and study the Word.

The Bible also says we must hide the Word in our hearts, so we might not sin against God. How can you hide the Word if you do not study or even read the Word of God? We are willing to engage in activities that fulfill the flesh with hours on social media, video games, gossip, idle time, and television. We develop excuses for why we do not have time to spend building our relationship and knowledge of Christ. We must be available for Bible study. Children rely on parents to teach them until they reach the age when they become accountable for their actions and knowledge. Before then, you are accountable for their biblical education.

The Bible says in Matthew 6:24 (AMP), "No one can serve two masters; for either he will hate the one and love the other, or he will be devoted to the one and despise the other. You cannot serve God and mammon [money, possessions, fame, status, or whatever is valued more than the Lord]."

Let us do what is needed to live a life in the light and not in darkness. And let us not deceive ourselves by believing we can do just enough, and God will accept that. You cannot build a relationship with anyone—including God—without a pursuit. Let me ask you, are you pursuing God? Are you curious about His attributes, promises, and desires for your future?

The Bible says in Jeremiah 29:11 (KJV),

> For I know the thoughts that I think toward you, saith the Lord, thoughts of peace, and not of evil, to give you an expected end. There is so much that God wants to share with us and if we do not commune with him, we will not get to know him. Pray and talk to God, read His word, and watch Him work in your life.

WAYS TO AVOID DECEPTION

We have talked about our roles as children of God and walking in the ways of Christ. I want to share some practical applications to avoid deception.

- Stay in Prayer: Pray without ceasing. This allows you to stay connected to Jesus, the power source, the Light of the world. No darkness and evil can abide in the Light.
- Stay in the Word: Read and study your Bible. The Word is a light unto my feet and a light unto my pathway. His words I have hidden in my heart that I might not sin against Him.
  Do not depend solely on what is being told to you during online sermons, in-person sermons, YouTube influencers, and the media. These methods must be tried and tested through the Word of God.
- Stay Armed: Put on the full armor of God, which will help you to withstand firmly this evil day.
  Name the pieces that make up the full armor of God. This can be found in the Bible, Ephesians, chapter 6 (armor and a weapon):

  o _____
  o _____
  o _____
  o _____
  o _____
  o _____
  o _____

- Stay Curious: Ask yourself and leadership questions. Here are some questions I ask myself: Does this message align with God's Word? Is this pastor or prophet asking me to pay for a Word from God? What does the Bible say about that?
- Stay in the Spirit: The Bible says we need to try the Spirit by the Spirit. This means that your "Holy Ghost radar" as my mom

would say, should be active and able to help you discern truths from schemes and trickery. The Holy Spirit will prick you if your spirit is contrary. You may even hear the voice of God. The Holy Ghost leads and guides you to all truths.

- Check the Fruit: You can tell a tree by the fruit it bears. A bad tree cannot produce good fruit. Nor can a good tree produce bad fruit. What type of fruit do you see? Stay away from the corrupt fruit. It is bad for your spiritual health! See Matthew 7:17 (KJV).

Write down how you currently or will implement these practical applications in your daily life:

_____

_____

_____

_____

_____

_____

Remember that if you are lacking in any area, you can pray and ask God to increase your understanding, your discernment, and your connection with Him to fine-tune your "radar." I continually ask God these things for myself. I desire to stay keen and sharp, avoid deception, and walk in the Light.

CONCLUSION

Living for Jesus is a choice. We are all accountable for our choices. I am so glad to know that if I have a heart of repentance, I can accept Jesus, live a wonderful life with Him, and reap all the benefits that come along with it. Divine protection, guidance, love, and a place in heaven with Him will be my portion, and it can be yours if you accept Jesus and live by His teachings.

I pray for the pastors, leaders, and ministries in the body of Christ, that all will stand firm on His Word, live His truths, preach His uncontaminated Word, and be ready to use the armor of God to stay protected from the enemy!

If we do not choose Jesus, there will be consequences. Remember the dream: You are on the road. Which way will you choose, the wide or narrow pathway? Heaven or hell? The Lord will not tolerate those who knowingly deny Him and walk contrary to His Word: "And since they did not see fit to acknowledge God *or* consider Him worth knowing [as their Creator], God gave them over to a depraved mind, to do things which are improper *and* repulsive" Romans 1:28 (AMP)

God has a remnant of those who will serve Him in these last days. Let us walk into the light! Keep striving to honor God with our lives and keep our focus during these perilous and dangerous times. We will see more and more calamities coming than we've ever seen before. Prepare! The great thing is we have hope! We have a Savior and a Comforter; we all have direct access to the Lord. Keep praying and reading God's Word. Ask questions; try the spirit by the Spirit of God. And stay armed with the armor of God. You will then uncover the fruit that one produces.

I humbly pray that this book has done what was intended, which is to enlighten, expose, and encourage. Thank you, and may God bless us all in our journeys in this life and ready us for the next. Amen.

ANSWER KEY

Here are the answers for the full armor of God:

- **Stay Armed**
  - o Belt of truth
  - o Helmet of salvation
  - o Feet shod with the gospel of peace
  - o Shield of faith
  - o Breastplate of righteousness
  - o Sword of the Spirit
  - o Weapon: prayer

Armor of God, Ephesians 6:10–18 (KJV)

Finally, my brethren, be strong in the Lord, and in the power of his might.

Put on the whole armour of God, that ye may be able to stand against the wiles of the devil.

For we wrestle not against flesh and blood, but against principalities, against powers, against the rulers of the darkness of this world, against spiritual wickedness in high places.

Wherefore take unto you the whole armour of God, that ye may be able to withstand in the evil day, and having done all, to stand.

Stand therefore, having your loins girt about with truth, and having on the breastplate of righteousness;

And your feet shod with the preparation of the gospel of peace;

Above all, taking the shield of faith, wherewith ye shall be able to quench all the fiery darts of the wicked.

And take the helmet of salvation, and the sword of the Spirit, which is the word of God:

Praying always with all prayer and supplication in the Spirit, and watching thereunto with all perseverance and supplication for all saints;

RESOURCES

King James and Amplified Version of the Holy Bible. www.Biblegateway.com.

Resource Link: Rinker, Dirk, and Jaffarian, Michael. *15 Million Americans Have Left Christianity In the Past 10 Years*, acstechnologies.com, retrieved July 27, 2022.

Merriam-Webster Online Dictionary.

ABOUT THE AUTHOR

Minister Shenoa T. Gibson, author of *Simple Steps to Salvation and Effective Prayer,* available on all digital platforms, was born and raised in Maryland. At age eleven, in 1987, she received the gift of the Holy Ghost. She participated in several youth choirs at the local church and within the Federation of Holy Trinity Churches. She has served as the youth and adult choir director, drummer, and Sunday school and vacation Bible school teacher. She served as the assistant church clerk for several years and on the Deaconess Board at the Northeast Holy Trinity Church, where they provided the foundation of spiritual necessities to ensure her growth in the Lord.

Minister Shenoa graduated from Laurel High School in 1994. She earned a degree at Prince George's Community College and a degree in business administration from Strayer University.

Her employment experience in the telecommunications industry was at Comcast and Verizon Wireless, which gave her more than twenty-five years of customer service and training and development experience. She currently works for a workforce development company.

She has served the underprivileged population in Prince George's County, Maryland, by connecting them to community resources needed for basic life necessities and helping them find employment to become self-sufficient. She worked as a supervisor in partnership with the Department of Social Services. She has returned to what she loves most, teaching and writing. She is also a regional trainer in workforce development and is growing as an independent business consultant.

Minister Shenoa prayed and was led by God to focus on developing and cultivating her prayer line ministry, Dare Two Pray. The ministry, started in July 2018, began when God showed His power by connecting two coworkers during a hardship, turning around a dire situation, and creating a miraculous praise report showing what the power of prayer can do when people get together in Jesus's name!

Minister Shenoa was ordained by the Christian Global Outreach Ministries in 2019. The mission of Dare Two Pray is to synchronize with women and men in unwavering faith, in one accord, with one mind, and with boldness approaching the throne of the Almighty God in prayer. The Dare Two Pray scripture theme is Ecclesiastes 4:12 (AMP): "A person standing alone can be attacked and defeated, but two can stand back-to-back and conquer. Three are even better, for a triple-braided cord is not easily broken." The ministry continues to grow with new callers, community work, and by witnessing God move in miraculous ways. With help from God, Minister Shenoa continues to witness to both great and small and will continue the work God has given her, striving for a crown of glory until her purpose has been fulfilled on this earth.

Printed in the United States
by Baker & Taylor Publisher Services

Printed in the United States
by Baker & Taylor Publisher Services